HOW TO LOVE:

SECRETS

TO

LASTING RELATIONSHIPS

By Jo Anne White, Ph.D.

Cover design by: Rachel Franklin

Warranty Disclaimer/Limits of Liability

This book is not intended to replace the services of a professional psychologist, counselor, or psychiatrist. It is intended for use by emotionally healthy persons with a desire to enhance their relationship and personal growth. The author and publishers make no warranty (expressed or implied) with respect to the suitability of this book for any particular personal situation of the user thereof. The author and publishers shall not be held liable for loss or any other damages including, but not limited to, special, consequential, incidental, or other damages. As always in the case of mental or emotional distress, seek the services of a competent professional.

This book contains materials protected under both United States and International Copyright Laws and Treaties. Any unauthorized use, printing, copying, electronic or other transfer, or any other distribution of this material is strictly prohibited under law.

TABLE OF CONTENTS

Introduction:

Relationships are like children. They need care, loving attention and commitment so that they can grow and be successful. You and your partner can create a relationship that is mutually satisfying and that will last.

Within this book are sound principles to help you keep your relationship fresh, loving and humming.

For over twenty years, I have counseled couples in search of how to make their relationships work and be more meaningful. Couples can grow apart, harbor resentments or disappointments that permanently damage the relationship.

The good news is that you can learn what's valuable to keep your new relationship strong and loving and each partner growing together.

You can have the relationship that you desire and you can make it happen right now as long as you both decide that you're in this special bond together. You can't do it without the support of your partner. A relationship demands the commitment of both of you.

Heed the advice. Practice the exercises and experience the love that can sustain difficult challenges, unexpected obstacles and weather the changes produced over time.

Please let me know how you're doing. I'd love to hear from you.

Jo Anne White, Ph.D.

Chapter One:
Love Struck

"Love at first sight is easy to understand; it's when two people have been looking at each other for a lifetime that it becomes a miracle."

Amy Bloom

Heartthrob:

Okay so you found someone that makes your heart turn somersaults whenever he or she's in view. And your thoughts always find their way back to your partner and with good reason. You are experiencing the early love jolts that we have when we fall in love.

Enjoy them and hope that you'll always feel good about that person. However, all the hoping in the world won't create a lasting, healthy relationship. But with conscious choice and action you can and you will.

Staying together is not a lofty goal. It takes desire, effort and commitment from both of you to keep the glow alive. In the early stages of love, you overlook a lot and can be blinded by your desire and by the excitement that you feel.

FEEL THE JOY, THE EXCITEMENT AND ALL THE WONDROUS EXPRESSIONS THAT YOUR LOVE WILL TAKE.

At the same time, remember that you have to return to earth at some point and when you do, reality sets in.

Fools Rush In:

When everything feels so good and so right, we want to go full speed ahead without any stops or breaks and be together all the time. BEWARE!

Remind yourself that you do have time and ask what's the rush all about? It takes time to learn about each other and to grow close and grow together. It takes time to find a rhythm together. And time to understand one another and to enjoy each other in different settings and different experiences.

Oh, I know how great it feels to be together and how you can't seem to concentrate on anything else; your mind is always on your partner. And with good reason.

When we feel good, our brains produce chemicals such as endorphins that make us feel even better. Your built-in mood elevator works beautifully and elevates your mood.

When your endorphins kick in, you feel good and you continue to feel good, even better than before. That feeling is also contagious to others; they feel good when they're around you.

If the relationship has all the right ingredients, it can evolve naturally over time. We don't really learn about another person in a flash. At first, we have our best foot forward.

Many of our personality flaws and shortcomings and those of our partner's are hidden from view but not forever.
Eventually, we will see the flaws (we all have them) and that's okay; no one is perfect!

Take your time to get to know your partner in many situations. Make sure that you don't steer so far away from your routine and from what's important to you.

You need to keep everything in your life moving forward along with the relationship. Don't get so caught up in love that you let your things go. You want to relieve stress and not create unnecessary stress. Stay on top of your game.

And remember don't ignore or discount the other valuable people and relationships that are in your life; they are still necessary and important.

Relationship Habits:

In the early stages of your relationship you are building good habits for the present and the future. Huh? Habits? You wonder how I can use that word when everything about your relationship is so bright and new.

Habits are just comfortable behaviors or actions that we repeat over and over. They become automatic over time. Okay, but what does that have to do with my relationship, you ask? Everything!

You are already practicing behaviors that will become familiar to both of you. They can set into a pattern and become a permanent part of the way you relate to each other so pay attention.

Be aware of what habits and patterns are forming in the relationship. In the early stages of your relationship, patterns are not set and can be easily changed. It's harder when those same behaviors have been going on for years and years.

Now you have a great opportunity to develop relationship habits that are healthy and make both of you feel good.

Breathing Room:

Just because you feel like you want to spend every waking moment with your special partner, please don't. Create some breathing room and time apart so that you don't stifle each other and burn up the relationship in record time. You'll have more to talk about when you're together, more to share and more to get excited about.

Remember when you are involved in other activities you generate new ideas and viewpoints. You have more to contribute in interest, conversation and personal growth that enhance your relationship.

Create time just for you so that you don't feel consumed and have more energy for you, your partner and your important priorities.

Hold Onto Your Friendships:

Now you have a partner and sadly the first to be shortchanged and set on the backburner are our friendships. Prevent that from that happening by paying attention. Know when you last contacted your close friends and make sure you keep up with them regularly.

You don't have to see a friend every week to feel connected. Your friends know you're busy; they are too.

The beauty of friendship is that friends understand and are tolerant of us sometimes more so than family. Keep up the contact with an e-mail, a phone call or a card and know that friendships can last a lifetime. And like everything else that's worthwhile, they need to be tended to and nourished. That's where you come in.

Make Time:

Show your friends they're important. Don't exclude them from your life because you believe that Mister Right just walked into your life. Mister Right may turn into Mister Wrong and leave.

Your friends can be there to help you through the difficult recovery but only if you haven't turned them away because you've been too busy. Make time for a friend in need and know that you can count on your friend in a heartbeat.

You may not have many evenings available because of your new love interest. That doesn't mean that you can't make time for a friend. Breakfast and lunch meetings are ideal ways to catch up on what's happening in your lives and share friendly confidences.

Scheduling time to walk with a friend or go to a spa or yoga class are ideal ways to nurture your friendships, your body and physical health at the same time.

Cultivate Your Interests:

How wonderful if you and your partner share many of the same interests. You'll have a lot to do together. In my experience as a therapist and coach, that's not always the way it really is, far from it.

More likely, you have your own interests and talents and so does he. Just because he's not into photography or yoga, doesn't mean that you have to give it up and not enjoy it. If you do, you may resent it and feel that you've sacrificed a significant part of you.

LOVE IS NOT REALLY ABOUT SACRIFICE. COOPERATION, COLLABORATION AND COMPROMISE, YES DEFINITELY!

But don't shortchange you just to make someone else happy. In the long run it won't work and you won't feel good. Instead you'll feel like there's something wrong and there is. You forgot to care for you!

When you are joyful and doing what feels and is worthwhile to you, you're better to be with. Not only are you happier, you are more appealing to your partner. You like yourself more.

Make sure that your relationship doesn't stifle you or that you don't have your beau on a tight rope. Both of you need to create the balance between alone time, other people time and 'us' time. Don't shortchange one for the other. If you see that's happening, change it.

Exercise 1: Why You Care:

Here's something to think about. Jot down what appeals to you about your partner. And while you're at it, find out what your partner likes about you.

This isn't an exercise to create friction, just the opposite. Know in the early stages of love and relationship why you're there.

There will always be more as the relationship grows and you have more experiences together but for now, find out what matters to you and to your partner.

Keep the list somewhere accessible and discuss your reasons with each other.

If you ever have a fleeting moment of niggling doubt, take out your list. Remember the reasons for your attraction and why you care.

What Attracts Me?

- _____
- _____
- _____
- _____
- _____

Chapter Two:
Don't Make Me Over

"Where love rules, there is no will to power; and where power predominates, there love is lacking. The one is the shadow of the other."

Carl Jung

If Only:

A large number of relationships don't survive after the first blush of romance. And often it's because we think that we can mold the person we're attracted to into something else, something more.

Oh, we like her alright but everything would be so much better if only she was more interested in sports so we could watch hockey or football games together on TV. If only he shared our enthusiasm for photography or theater, life would be grand.

Or maybe he can't seem to be on time and more often than not, he keeps you waiting.

Maybe you wish he was a better dresser or a better dancer. Maybe her boisterous behavior when you're out with friends is embarrassing to you. And oh, her cooking leaves much to be desired!

However, any behavior that feels unkind, disrespectful or maligns you must be addressed. The treatment of you or mistreatment of you is not negotiable or tolerable. Never!

So make sure you are taken care of physically, emotionally and mentally in the relationship. No mind games, please! Forget the excuses from you or from him. When it comes to your well-being and your personal safety, you don't compromise.

No Makeovers Please:

If you're out to change him and make him into something that conforms to your lifestyle, forget it. That's the beginning of the end for many couples. Instead, relish the differences between the two of you and accept who she is. After all, that's what attracted you to her in the first place.

You can buy your love a sweater or shirt for his birthday and offer him different choices, selecting what your preferences are. Make sure he's open to them. You are making suggestions not schooling him so don't ram them down his gullet. He needs to be receptive.

And you both may need to learn tolerance and patience.

FITTING TOGETHER AS A COUPLE NOT ONLY TAKES TIME, IT TAKES PRACTICE.

Keep practicing!

Stay Alert:

I often hear from troubled couples about the behaviors or traits their partners have that are disappointing and upsetting to them. More often than not, these behaviors were there in the beginning of the relationship but were overlooked.

You have choices no matter what stage your relationship is at. In your new relationship, don't ignore what's important to you. Some behaviors and values you can live with and some you really have to draw the line on. Only you know what interferes with the ability to stay close and what goes against your values.

Values:

Your values are the beliefs and guidelines by which you live and are deeply connected to the core or essential part of who you are. They are not to be taken lightly.

Often the values you hold are the beliefs you've been raised with. You can choose to go against them. Those learned family values are embraced or replaced with what is more compatible with who you are.

When you enter into a new relationship, there are specific traits of your partner that appeal. The attraction may be the person's looks, sense of humor, how she treats you, how confident he is or any number of reasons and personal characteristics.

Values are not always apparent unless we're in a situation where they're expressed or unless we ask.

You need to know what your values are even if they're still evolving and they are evolving as long as you're alive.

Values are difficult to compromise and it's important to learn what your partner's values are. You need to know if there's a good fit between your values and his.

23

Don't underestimate the importance of values and truly consider if your values and your partner's are compatible over time.

Values can include views and beliefs regarding the rearing and treatment of children, monogamy, family, spirituality, shared interests, time together and so much more.

Many couples think that values aren't as important as how they feel about each other. Yet, more often breakups occur when the values of each partner conflict and there isn't a way to compromise.

Mismatched:

A partner may be intolerant or prejudiced to others which strike a nerve in you because of your sensitivity to others. You appreciate diversity and the wide differences in people and feel uncomfortable with his behavior.

A partner who takes fidelity or honesty lightly when those values are high on your list may not be a good match for you over time. Not only will you feel discomfort, you may get hurt because of the mismatch.

Love doesn't have to be deaf and blind. You have the right and the need to know and to explore how your partner thinks and what's important to him. Find out if you can live with her values and if she can live with yours.

You Choose:

And remember, especially when love is newest and you are really just finding out about each other, you have a choice. You are choosing a partner to be in a relationship with. And that choice needs to be made with conscious intent.

Get off that cloud, rip off your blinders and listen to what you are hearing. Know what you're experiencing in your new love. Pay attention.

Know what you want in a love partner and go after it. If you realize early on that the relationship has "doom" written all over it because of major differences, get out.

"All love that has not friendship for its base is like a mansion built upon sand."

Ella Wheeler Wilcox

Acceptance:

Okay, so you can live with his values and sometimes you agree to disagree. That's great. Now you have a challenge ahead of you. You have to accept his quirks and annoying little habits whatever they are and visa versa.

Good luck trying to change her. You'll wear out by the effort. Her constant need to talk disarms you and you fade out. You need to reach a place of peace with the quirks and shortcomings of your partner. Or forever brood or complain.

As strange as it seems, often when couples fight, the little things set them off. Leaving the cap off the toothpaste, messiness, need for order, lateness or forgetfulness are the ammunition.

Acceptance is the alternative. Do you know people who don't want to be accepted and appreciated for who they are? Not likely. Admit you want the same treatment; we all do. And you have to give it right back to your mate.

ACCEPTANCE OF YOUR PARTNER CAN OPEN THE
DOOR TO TRUE INTIMACY.

You feel safe to be who you are and to share more of you with
him. But it doesn't always come easily. You have to keep at it.

Exercise 2: Values and Beliefs:

◈ **Examine the important values that you have. Write them down.**

◈ **Find out what values are dear to your partner.**

◈ **Discuss your values and how they can strengthen your relationship.**

◈ **What mutual values do you share that you can build on?**

Chapter Three: Communication & Word Power

"Love must be as much a light as it is a fire."

Henry David Thoreau

What Say You?

Communication is basic to any relationship. Words have power. Body language and behavior also let your partner know how you think and feel. Even silence commands attention.

Make sure you communicate what you want to clearly and with compassion. Your biggest hurdle is that you probably communicate much differently than she or he does.

Not surprising, your brains aren't wired the same way. Men and women have different styles of communication. You have to adjust to the differences to survive and thrive together.

You might have to first learn how to communicate to him or her. Imagine that you both come from different cultures. To understand each other you must find common ground.

Females remember and rehash all the related past with the present. He responds like he's been attacked and the schism widens between them.

Ladies, keep it simple and stick to the moment and the *now* agenda to be heard. Save the longwinded talk for your girlfriends.

And guys don't tune out. Women want to know that you're paying attention and value what they say.

What is Your Communication IQ?

1. Are you an active listener?

2. Do you wait until your partner finishes speaking before you speak?

3. Do you communicate without blame?

4. Is your communication compassionate?

5. What does your body language signal to your partner?

6. Do you give your partner feedback?

7. Do you communicate with empathy by putting yourself in your partner's place with respect to his/her feelings?

8. Do you speak in 'I' terms and not in accusations?

9. Do you take responsibility for your feelings and your words?

Avoid the Blame:

Blaming only puts your partner on the defensive and makes it harder to relate. And always seeing the glass half-empty won't improve your outlook or the relationship.

Ready to attack with fault-finding and negative verbal assault won't bring you two closer. And if you feel good afterwards, it won't last. Usually, you feel worse because you don't like who you've become when you're unpleasant and spewing venom.

Yes, get your feelings out. Express your needs and concerns but do it in a way that causes the least harm. Learn together how to share that information openly and without attack or blame.

And keep a sense of humor about you. Your partner isn't the enemy, only from a different world. Learning his language, customs and culture takes time and patience.

Ask for what you want and expect to get it. Rather than complain, let him know clearly what you'd like to happen. You don't always have to be right; you do have to learn to speak up and also listen openly to what your partner says.

If you're spending more time blaming and fault-finding than loving and appreciating each other, something's not right. In a new relationship you both have to step back and examine the way you communicate.

You may have to change your approach. Or maybe what you feel is an internal signal that something's not right about the relationship altogether and you've been denying that to yourself.

"Love and kindness are never wasted. They always make a difference. They bless the one who receives them and they bless you the giver."

Barbara De Angelis

Deliver Kindness:

All relationships require some effort and you're not going to agree on every detail even if you want to. What is important is that you communicate and are clear about your needs and his and what matters.

Exercising kindness and being open to handle disagreements amicably and being able to bend when necessary are traits that encourage cooperation and union.

Sometimes demonstrating what we need to our partner is worth a million words. Treat her the way you'd like to be treated. Kind actions and gestures show our love and caring and can boost our partner's self-esteem.

Not everything in a relationship is equal and doesn't have to be. Throw out your score card. Remember that you do things for him because you want to and because you feel good when you do.

Don't always expect something back in return. Yes, getting your needs met is important but expectations are relationship busters. Expecting your partner to be a certain way and always wanting proof of her love can diminish what you have.

Problem Solving:

You may wonder what problem solving has to do with getting along with your partner.

Many people have not learned or practiced effective strategies to handle their everyday problems, especially the unexpected ones.

And now there are two of you and you find that when dilemma hits, the old resources you've used before don't work. Now you have to be aware of how to solve it together.

If you handle problems by avoidance or denial or bolting when things get sticky and uncomfortable, you can put the relationship in jeopardy. Conversely, if your strategies include always needing be right or faulting the other person, you may have to change your tune. Take responsibility for your role.

When you care about each other, your mutual goal is to keep the relationship alive and well. It needs to be the winner in any argument and come out on top without too many bruises. Learning to disagree fairly is essential.

Express anger or disappointment without sacrificing loving behavior. Accept your partner's anger in comfort and without retaliation. Maintain kindness and fairness throughout.

With two different approaches, you need patience and resolution that bring the best possible outcome to the situation and to both of you. Running and blaming are out. Lively, open discussion and active and empathic listening are in. So listen up.

"Love does not consist of gazing at each other but in looking together in the same direction."

Antoine De Saint-Exupery

Listen Well:

Listening with empathy means that you place yourself in your partner's shoes or experience to understand how she feels. Sometimes it's important to just do that. And reflect back to her what she's communicated. Having our feelings understood and appreciated means a lot.

When you are listening, really listen. Minimize the distractions and interruptions. Give your partner your undivided attention. If you are biased, you're already armed with your next retort to back up your viewpoint only. And not attending to what he said.

So really pay attention and try to let go of the pre-judgments that get in the way of you hearing his views.

An impatient listener can't wait to get the next word in and often ends up interrupting before the person's finished. Your intention is to promote harmony in communication.

Impatience is a killer that produces disharmony and discourtesy. Instead, be patient without being passive. Listen well but be responsive. Give feedback and understanding or appreciation of what your partner said.
Always, always, ask her to clarify if you don't understand.

Negotiations:

Relationships work best when you negotiate. This week, you go to the restaurant of your choice. Next week, it's hers. Divide the labor and home tasks the same way. Make mutual decisions that make both of you feel satisfied.

No longer assume traditional roles unless they're comfortable for you. In many households, the man cooks and is home with the children. Sharing responsibility and negotiating make for happier times. Resentment won't build up. Each person feels that his/her contribution is worthwhile and appreciated.

Discuss openly the best way to come to an agreement which is really what you want. To feel good in a relationship both of you need to get your needs met and feel satisfied. Create a sense of balance and fairness in your communications and agreements.

YOU AND YOUR PARTNER WILL FEEL THE BALANCING EFFECTS OF HEALTHY LOVING COMPROMISE.

Compromise:

Compromise doesn't mean that you always get your way or that you always give in to what he wants because it's easier than discussing what's important. You recognize the necessity for give and take in your relationship. To do that, you honor and respect the differences in both of you.

The goal is accommodation, accommodating your needs and wishes and his so that both of you can feel satisfied.

Understanding and compassion fuel compromise. Keep a desire to create a win-win situation between you and your partner as often as possible. Be reasonable with your expectations and your willingness to see and accept his/her viewpoint without a lot of judgment.

Reach agreements through discussion and sharing. Air your feelings and be clear about your views. You aim is to reach a decision that you're both happy with and that brings you closer together.

"Love is a condition in which the happiness of another person is essential to your own."

Robert Heinlein

Mutual Respect:

All relationships from business to love partnerships demand respect. When we become comfortable and familiar around our partner, we may want to drop the niceties, the formalities of please and thank-you, the common courtesies. You may want to, but don't!

They are there to remind us that the person who is with us is entitled to the same respect and common courtesy that we afford others. The one you love should not be shortchanged in this area.

And so often, I see mutual respect break down. What once started as a joke, a familiar slur, gets out of hand and someone gets hurt. Don't make the same mistake.

Mutual respect and consideration are the highest compliments we can give to our partner. That and our love command respect in return.

When we generate a message of acceptance and we hold our loved ones in esteem, their feeling of value expands.

42

Exercise 3: MUTUAL RESPECT

Write down separately and discuss with your partner, how you demonstrate mutual respect.

How do you communicate best with other? What is your communication style?

Discuss how you both handle disagreements and resolve conflicts?

Talk about how both of you can improve your ways of dealing with conflict.

Tryout the suggestions you've both decided on. Keep trying until you get it right and you both feel valued even during a conflict.

Chapter Four:
Intimacy

"You learn to speak by speaking, to study by studying, to run by running, to work by working, and just so you learn to love by loving."

Saint Francis De Sales

The Love We Crave:

Intimacy is not just about sex. Sexuality has its place in the intimate bond shared with a special partner. But alone, it's not enough and leaves us lacking and wanting more. More what? We seek more acceptance, closeness and shared moments when we can feel safe and okay to be what we are.

Intimacy is physical and emotional closeness and is not always easy to sustain. Some of us fear and avoid intimacy because of the pain and hurt of past relationships.

Intimacy is shared feelings. An open expression of what you are and what bothers you and makes you joyful when you're together. It's not just shared "I Love Yous".

Intimacy includes the deep-down unpleasant, negative feelings such as fear and resentment that often get buried and unexpressed.

We have been taught to stuff these feelings way down. We hide them from our partner so we don't get hurt. Or so we don't hurt him. Without taking the risk, we never really get heard. And the build-up of tension is never released inside us.

When we feel safe and secure, we can risk expressing our feelings and risk being heard.

Get Real With Intimacy:

How do you know when there's real intimacy? Intimacy is real when it allows for honest and open dialogue without fear of backlash, recrimination, guilt or emotional and physical harm.

A green light is on for us to feel secure and take risks to truly express our feelings when we create an environment of loving acceptance.

When we love, we are vulnerable. Our hearts are open and we feel tender and can be easily bruised by our partner's inconsideration or lack of understanding. Make sure in your relationship that you both recognize and are sensitive to each other's vulnerability.

WHEN YOU FEEL SAFE, YOU MORE EASILY EXPRESS WHAT'S ON YOUR MIND AND IN YOUR HEART AND AREN'T AFRAID OF REPRISAL OR RIDICULE.

47

Trust:

Without trust, the relationship cannot grow. Yet trust is not just something that automatically happens. It takes time to build and strengthen trust between you. Trust involves mutual commitment and honest expression of what is taking place in you and with him.

It's important for each partner to realize that trust is earned. Trust takes time. You can't rush it but you can take conscious action to build it.

Your partner will trust you more easily when you do what you say. Don't make your words empty. Follow up your words with action that matches them. You're more believable and reliable when your words and actions are consistent with each other. The guesswork is removed when we are sincere.

The ABC's of Trust

1. Trust doesn't happen overnight.

2. Trust is earned.

3. Trust is heartfelt.

4. Trust is the honest expression of what both of you are experiencing and feeling.

5. In trust, words and actions match each other.

6. In trust, you are sincere.

7. In trust, the guesswork is gone.

Let Your Intentions Be Known:

Make sure that you communicate your intentions so that there is no misunderstanding, judgment or false assumptions.

Our partners are uneasy when we are indirect and round-about. That kind of noncommittal behavior leaves room for doubts. False conclusions are drawn that increase her distrust rather than foster it.

And why do it? If your goal is a loving successful relationship, hiding behind inconsistencies and half-truths will only undermine and chisel away at true loving.

Silence is damaging to a relationship and leaves room for distrust and doubt. When we are close with our partner, we feel safe. And it's okay to share what is real about us without fear of recrimination, guilt, physical or emotional payback.

We are open to hear our partner's truth even if we don't agree with it. By doing so, we create an emotional climate that fosters trust and stands behind truth.

Acceptance:

Honesty and openness are important to create mutual acceptance. You don't have to like everything about your partner but you do need to accept who he is in spite of your differences. At some point his quirks and annoying behaviors surface as do yours. The tendency is towards disapproval which creates roadblocks to closeness.

You can run away in dismay or learn tolerance and acceptance. Remind yourself that seeking perfection is unrealistic. You want what she wants. You desire your partner's approval and to be lovingly accepted for you. And that includes all your imperfections and strange tendencies.

In acceptance, you let go of the need to change her. Rather than manipulate or control, you find a way to emphasize his positive qualities. You practice tolerance and patience.

Learn to accept and love yourself more. Don't find fault with him when there are glaring similarities between the two of you.

What you dislike in you may show up in him as well. Those same uncomfortable traits reflect back at you as in a mirror.

PRACTICE LOVING YOURSELF WITHOUT CONDITIONS. AND IT WILL BE EASIER TO UNCONDITIONALLY ACCEPT HIS SHORTCOMINGS.

Conflict Resolution:

How you and your partner resolve disagreements is an important part of intimacy. You have choices here. Not every relationship runs smoothly all the time.

You are two different people coming together and will not see eye to eye on everything and that's fine.

However, how you argue affects how you feel about each other over time. Hateful slurs and angry behavior can erode the intimacy in your relationship so you need to be careful and gentle with each other.

Set some ground rules and stick to them. Talk about what irks you and how you can best handle disagreement without going off or saying hurtful words that you can't take back. The best time to talk it over is not in the heat of an argument.

Make It Okay To Be Vulnerable:

Remember, when you care about each other, you're both vulnerable. You need your partner to treat you with loving kindness. Be sensitive to what buttons you push in her. If possible, maintain eye contact throughout the disagreement.

We all have emotional scars from the past and triggers that continue to hurt and inflame us. That's part of being human.

Agree to find concrete ways to come to a resolution swiftly and as painlessly as possible.
Don't seethe quietly and don't allow arguments to fester. They don't need to become ugly, drawn-out affairs.

Remind yourself that keeping the relationship healthy and happy is as much about how you fight as the good times you have together.

Fight fairly and resolve arguments constructively. Stick to the situation at hand and don't dredge up everything that went wrong in the relationship. Make sure that you handle each disagreement as it comes up. And don't allow for resentment and distance to grow like a wedge between the two of you.

Love Safely:

When you're in the middle of a charged conflict, it's important to keep it safe for both of you. Of course, there will be issues that come up in any relationship. Decide in advance to handle them without blame or criticism.

All criticism and blame do is put your partner on the defensive. They defeat the goal of being close. Defensiveness creates distance between you. And distance can lead to separation.

Criticism won't change his behavior. He changes with positive encouragement and when he feels good about you and about himself. Lavish praise on him but be sincere. Don't just make it up.

Reward the positive and loving actions she takes when they happen. Do it with praise, affection and touch. Let him know when he's doing something right. If he feels goods about it, he'll repeat the action.

Remember why you chose her and choose her over and over again.

55

Own your feelings and take responsibility for them. Conflict creates tension and stress and you need to find ways to handle them. Expressing your feelings constructively and with love can avoid upset and misunderstanding. Give your partner the room and the okay to do the same.

Be Forgiving:

She may do or say things you don't like. You may argue. Sometimes you're wrong, sometimes he's lax and forgetful. Inconsistencies happen, mistakes happen. They happen in the best of relationships. Forgiveness and understanding can make them right.

If you're wrong, own up to it and apologize. Admitting your mistakes goes a long way to clear the air and allows you and your partner to feel good again.

If the mistake is on the other foot, accept his apology. Be forgiving and get over your injured feelings as quickly as possible. Don't hold onto grudges for eternity. Try to resolve whatever gets in the way of your closeness and practice forgiveness all the time.

Gratitude is Gratifying:

She wants to know that you appreciate what she's done. The special meal she made just for you or choosing a shirt you favor. He likes to hear a thank you from you when he spends money.

It doesn't matter if those kind and generous acts are repeated hundreds and thousands of times. Every time you express gratitude for those deeds makes it seem like the first time.

Show your appreciation for your partner's efforts. Acknowledge them. They don't have to be great to warrant your gratitude. Sometimes it's the little sentimental acts that affect us the most. Cherish them and let your partner know that you do as often as possible.

There are never enough "Thank-yous" or "I'm sorrys" between the two of you. And sometimes they make all the difference in ending a disagreement with love.

Being gracious is polite and it tells her that you're aware of her kindness. It's a way to recognize rather than just expect him to do for something for you.

Throw away the expectations that can erode true intimacy. Yes, get your needs met but don't come to the relationship with a long heavy list of rules and what he's supposed to do for you. Discover what you both like together and always keep the communication open.

Mutual Goals:

It's important to have goals that you strive for together. They can range from outings to shared activities to purchases to long range planning about home and family. They can be spiritual goals, educational goals, communication goals and health goals.

The idea is that you come together in planning, in discussing and in keeping these goals in your minds and work together to make them happen.

Being goal oriented is good not just personally but also for the relationship. Discuss where you'd like the relationship to go and have goals to strive for. Mutual goals can be relationship affirming and bring the two of you closer.

True Intimacy:

Imbalances in the relationship can interfere with true intimacy. Relationships are not power-plays where one person is viewed as more important than the other. Respect your partner's work, time and feelings. Recognize them to be as valuable as your own.

That doesn't mean that we ignore each partner's different strengths and knowledge. The emphasis is on equality rather than undermining or disrespecting our partner. Of course there will be differences but honor them and cherish them.

Intimacy is reflected in body language, touch, laughter, verbal sharing and making time for each other. Touch such as hugging and kissing add to those feelings of warmth and connection.

But true intimacy makes us feel treasured and safe. We feel good about us because there is someone who truly appreciates and cherishes who we are.
When we have those kinds of feelings, we feel like we're home.

True Intimacy

1. You feel safe and treasured.

2. You feel respected.

3. The emphasis is on equality.

4. Communication is open and valued.

5. Differences are appreciated.

6. Each person is recognized for who he/she is.

7. When the going gets tough, you stay together and fight for the relationship.

8. Forgiveness and gratitude share an important place in your relationship.

9. You are acknowledged for your efforts and so is your partner.

Exercise 4: Grow in Intimacy

Write down ways that you and your partner express intimacy.

Discuss ways to improve the intimacy you share.

What other ways can you both demonstrate acceptance and appreciation?

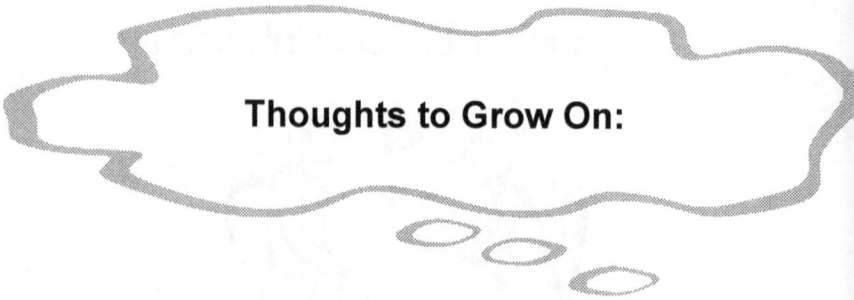

Thoughts to Grow On:

1. Think about how you enrich your partner.

2. Think about how your partner enriches you and your life.

3. What else can you do to enrich your partner? Do it!

4. What else can your partner do to enrich you? Ask for it!

5. In what ways do you include each other in your respective lives?

6. How can you include each other more?

Chapter Five:
Keep It New

"Love is the expansion of two natures in such fashion that each include the other, each is enriched by the other."

Felix Adler

New Beginnings:

In the beginning of a relationship it's easy to have romance, playfulness and fantasy. That's when passion, newness and the excitement of getting to know each other reel us in. And it's wonderful. Yet, somewhere along the way, if we stop paying attention, they all get buried under mindless routine.

Responsibilities and habits claim center stage. The vitality of the relationship is sucked out. And only a while before, we were filled with passion and enchantment for our partner. What went wrong?

We find ourselves going to the same restaurants, going out with the same people, having the same conversations and even the same arguments. We give into monotony because it takes less effort or at least we think it does.

We get comfortable with ways of relating that dull the relationship rather than enhance and enliven it. Break the routine and decide to do something different.

In the long run, there are no shortcuts to getting to know and deeply love someone. The way to keep your relationship strong and alive, no matter how new or old, is to grow it.

Yes, you have to grow your relationship like a flower or plant. New and old relationships built to last have some elements in common. Foremost is the commitment to the relationship, to one another and to you. If you prepare now, you can be worry-free.

Prepare Now:

Yes, you need to be mindful of what's going on in the relationship. Keep all your senses open and be aware of your role in the interactions. Relationships aren't always fifty-fifty but they do need the give and take of each partner. Both partners willingly contribute to a successful relationship.

There is ebb and flow in every relationship. They have high points and low points, growth spurts and quiet times when you both are apart yet connected. A relationship is organic like all other living things. Therefore, relationships require care, unique attention and whatever else to make them strong, healthy, lively and lasting.

RELATIONSHIPS THRIVE BEST WHEN THERE ARE TWO WILLING, OPEN PEOPLE WHO HAVE A RESPONSIBILITY TO THEMSELVES AND TO EACH OTHER.

They also recognize and act on mutual responsibility to their love.

As each person grows and blossoms so does the relationship. Each of you grows separately and together as a couple.

The challenge is to grow differently without growing apart.

You can include feel-good ways that nurture the relationship and your partner. Practice attentiveness and avoid neglect.

Show you Care:

Caring for another is effort. Yet acts of love feel good to both the giver and the person who receives them. There are so many ways to show you care and many of them are inexpensive but powerful. Get your message across.

Here are just a few. Devise your own caring program
and put it into action.
You'll both be glad that you did.

1. Call or text message whenever you're going to be late. Don't keep her guessing
2. Cultivate loyalty
3. Remember important events
4. Be affectionate
5. Make him laugh
6. Do some chore or task to make her job easier
7. Plan for time together and stick to it
8. Be attentive to your partner
9. Participate willingly in an activity that he/she is passionate about

Nurture Your Partner:

To be nurtured is to be cared for and given the necessary ingredients to thrive. What does that mean for both of you? It means everything that we've been talking about throughout this book and more. Good communication, politeness, kindness, fair fighting, shared feelings and intimate moments, respect, trust, honesty and commitment are all important.

There are also fun and breezy ways to nourish your partner. Run a bath for her. Massage each other with oils. Give each other special gifts. You don't have to incur a lot of expense to make her happy. Plan an outing with him in mind. Surprise each other.

WHATEVER YOU DO, MAKING LOVE STRONG IS A CHOICE THAT YOU ACTIVELY MAKE OVER AND OVER.

You need to renew the relationship all the time so it doesn't get old or neglected.

Despite your busy schedules, let him know that he's important by planning time together. You have to put energy and time into the relationship to keep it.

Fourteen Ways to Nurture Your Partner:

1. Find a book at a bookstore that he'll appreciate.

2. Buy her feline a cat toy.

3. Stock up on his favorite munchies.

4. Send a love note or I miss you card.

5. Compliment your partner.

6. Show appreciation.

7. Exude kindness.

8. Make him laugh.

9. Give a massage.

10. Receive a massage.

11. Plan a candlelight dinner.

12. Call her in the middle of the day just to say hello.

13. Stick a love note in his pocket or briefcase.

14. Validate and appreciate your partner whenever you can.

Be romantic:

Females aren't the only people who enjoy romance. There are so many ways to be romantic. Nowadays you have a lot of romance support through the Internet. There are also companies delighted to help you come up with something special for her. And not just on her birthday, your anniversary or Valentine's Day.

Romance can include holding hands, necking, buying flowers, sharing your favorite meal together and planning a date at the place you first met. I've only covered a few. Talk it over with your partner and find out what's romantic to him. You'll be surprised. Maybe it's a night home with the two of you curled up together and watching an old movie. While you're at it, let him know what tugs at your heart strings.

What do you consider romantic?
What about your partner?
Talk it over and find out!

Affirm your partner:

Be generous with sincere compliments and positive ways to make your partner feel good about her. Whether it's her looks, something she's done, said or achieved, acknowledge it. That strengthens the bond between you and adds to her confidence and self-esteem.

Let him know that you value what he does for you. Spell out what you appreciate about him and often. We can't get enough of the good stuff. And we've all been programmed with negative messages. Make a difference.

Vow to celebrate the positive actions and behaviors of both of you. Be supportive with affirming her goodness and with constant confirmation of your love.

When you validate him, you also validate yourself and your choice of a partner.

Stay Connected:

You are both so busy. There are separate meetings, separate responsibilities and separate time-out. That's fine, even healthy. However, in the midst of your busyness and all the different activities, stay connected and make time for each other.

Even if it's a phone message just to say hello or to share something special about your day or about that business meeting. Making your partner aware of how your day is and how you feel keeps up the connection between the two of you and feels good.

Keep up the contact. Maintain the communication. You'll be glad you did. Relationships can get lost through busyness and lack of attention. You can prevent that by staying in touch and often.

Plan on some activities you can do together. Make time for intimacy and create intimate moments. Physically affirm your love with handholding, touching and kissing.

Touching is such an important way to remain connected. It feels good and warm to both of you and deepens the intimacy that you share. Touching demonstrates support and is an offering of comfort. Be comforting and supportive to your partner and touch more often.

Increase Pleasure:

We all like to feel good. Increasing pleasure in the relationship is both in the giving and receiving of it. Knowing, if you don't already know what gives him pleasure is important. Share with him what is pleasurable to you.

I'm not just speaking of sexual pleasure, although that's important. And it's okay to talk about and even demonstrate what pleases you in the bedroom. That is as long as you don't make him feel like an inadequate caveman, all thumbs and no style or technique.

Find gentle and loving ways to express sexual needs. Your partner is not in your life so you can exploit her. Talking about sex may be uncomfortable at first but it will get easier. And it's worth it. Sometimes just talking it over will do wonders for intimacy in all its expressions.

Lighten Up:

You work hard to earn a living and juggle your life. So make time to play together and have fun. That's what keeps all relationships young and novel. Find ways to laugh and laugh together and don't take everything so seriously.

Your relationship can use a dose of fun. Here's where you can be silly and inventive. Plan on the unusual, the decadent and the off-the-beaten path kind of moments when you can revel in your playfulness and laugh at your silliness.

Be spontaneous and try-on something different. Whether it's a mystery night out or something new in the kitchen or the bedroom, make sure that it's mutually satisfying. The goal here is to banish boredom and feel good so it has to be something that agrees with you both.

Invest in Quality Time:

We all need alone time. And you have to be okay with those moments that he spends by himself and with his friends. Think of them as time for him to renew and recharge. And plan for your own time of renewal.

Yet, for a relationship to last, investing in quality time together is essential. Decide what that means for you. For some couples, quality time includes moments when they go to church or synagogue or meditate together. Spiritual time can also be walks in nature.

A characteristic of quality time is that it's shared time apart from routine. It happens when you're both involved and paying attention. Quality time can be physical or when you're actively sharing your views. You decide what makes it quality time and make it an important part of your schedule.

Celebrate Your Love:

Having a loving relationship that is satisfying and supports each of you is the best reason to celebrate. Make up ways to celebrate your love and each other.

Here are a few ideas. Invent your own.

- Exchange cards often that express your love and appreciation.
- Keep track of special days and anniversaries that are yours; make them romantic and loving.
- Find a theme song you both enjoy that expresses your love and relationship.
- Call her just to let her know you care or enjoy her company.
- Woo each other often.
- Let him know he's special by cooking his favorite dinner with candle light.
- Bestow compliments on him/her that are sincere and heartfelt.
- Do 'just because' deeds that make him feel special and demonstrate your feelings.

Celebrate You:

A hardy relationship relies on the strength of the two people. That means taking responsibility for your own well-being and includes your physical, emotional, mental and spiritual health.

Your job is to grow and evolve and be the best that you can be. By taking care of you, you add to the relationship. Find ways to de-stress, to work through your feelings and stay on track with your goals and dreams.

Just because you're in a relationship doesn't mean that you forfeit what is really important to you. Keep yourself fit in mind, body and spirit and nurture yourself.

When you feel good, you convey that to your partner and the relationship prospers.

Be kind, loving and sincere and prosper!

Exercise 5A: Celebrate Your Partner

Part I:

1. Make a list of what gives you pleasure that your partner can do for you.
2. Be playful and inventive and sincere.
3. Share the list with your partner. This is best when both partners complete the activity.
4. Take turns carrying out what's on the list.

Exercise 58: Celebrate Your Love

Part II:

1. Discuss ways that you and your partner will celebrate your special love.
2. Mark dates on your calendar or day timers to follow through with the celebration.
3. Have Fun.
4. Do it again and again but always make it special and extraordinary.

Chapter Six:
Grow Your Relationship

"I believe that imagination is stronger than knowledge – myth is more potent than history – dreams are more powerful than facts – hope always triumphs over experience – laughter is the cure for grief – love is stronger than death."

Robert Fulghum

Friends and Lovers:

Many people believe that it's okay to be in love with someone without friendship. Often, at the start of a relationship, raw passion leads the way. Passion is wonderful in all its forms!

By itself, passion is not enough for a lasting relationship. Unless that's all you want; then there you have it. And that's fine when both partners agree.

But you want more or you wouldn't be reading this book. Friendship adds warmth and loyalty and gives your relationship more depth. And to keep your relationship alive, it must grow in many ways.

With our close friends, we laugh and share and enjoy each other's company. We confide in each other and hold each other dear. We do what we can to care for them and to keep the friendship.

Even when there are disagreements or hurt feelings, we don't turn our backs. Instead, we get through them because our friends are important and we want them in our lives.

Weather the Storms:

Your partnership also needs those qualities of true and lasting friendship. And you don't run when it gets tough or even uncomfortable. Sometimes the relationship is strained because of outside elements like death and lay-offs, sickness and financial challenges not anticipated. Sometimes the strain comes from inside.

The feelings and actions of you both affect the relationship. Let's face it, we all have ups and downs; that's what makes us human. It's our response to them that makes all the difference. It's a choice that you make over and over again. You choose to wade through them, to stay and not leave.

Keep in mind that there are always bumps in the road and not every day is smooth sailing. Yet to stay afloat, you don't run at the first storm or any strong wind that shakes up the relationship.

Lasting Relationships:

In lasting relationships, it's going through the challenges together that builds the relationship and draws you both closer. You learn with each challenge and with time passing that you can get through each difficulty together.

As a team, you do it successfully. That boosts your confidence in you and him. You also feel confident in the solidness of what you have together.

And as you weather each storm together, you learn new skills that you didn't know you had.

Or you hone the skills you already had. With each new challenge handled, there is satisfaction and a sense of victory that the two of you share.

After all, you've done it successfully together. What a wonderful feat and reason to celebrate your love.

Choose the Relationship:

Below is a list of twelve keys to keep the relationship healthy, vibrant and alive. Come up with your own list of what you believe goes into a lasting relationship. Do it separately and together as a couple when the time is right.

Use any of the elements in this book that you both think are important to keep your relationship strong. And add others that you come up with. You aren't limited. Talk them over with your partner.

In this book you read about important characteristics to keep your love partnership alive and running smoothly with the ability to weather any storm. Don't just take my word for it.

Read through it again when you're ready. And do the exercises, separately and with your partner. They will enhance communication and cooperation.

By openly expressing what you both need and what the relationship needs every step of the way, there is steadiness and direction. There are no surprises about what's happening to both of you and to the relationship. Keep the surprises for the fun things to do to spice up your relationship.

Twelve Keys to A Lasting Relationship:

Love

Honesty

Trust

Communication

Appreciation

Mutual Respect

Commitment

Friendship

Sharing and Together Time

Fairness

Forgiveness

Playfulness

Growing Together:

Although there are important elements to growing together, the magic formula lies in the commitment the two of you have. It's a commitment to make your relationship work. This means teamwork and not giving up. Not even if you want to because your relationship has plunged to an all-time low.

Giving up is easy and can be avoided if you both decide to consciously grow together by blending time spent together and time spent apart. You are in a relationship not to be held back but to be all that you can be and more... Relationships that last enhance each person.

By Growing Separately:

Growing together is to also grow separately. You have different interests, talents, dreams, skills and experiences. You have a responsibility to you to cultivate them throughout your life. Cultivate your interests with you in mind and ask for encouragement and support from your partner.

Your partner has a responsibility to cultivate his interests also. While you're doing that, you are also sharing interests, dreams and activities that you create together. They can change as you change and grow.

Remember to give your partner the space and the support he needs for his growth. Holding back a person you love doesn't only hurt him. That hurts and undermines the relationship too.

Fear of losing her may be one reason but it only creates distance and resentment between you. Release your fear and take a chance on love.

LOVE CHOOSES TO STAY WHEN THERE IS
PERMISSION FOR GROWTH TO TAKE PLACE.

And don't hold yourself back for the same reason. Instead, encourage you both to move ahead and reach for new heights.

Growing Physically:

This seems obvious but why aren't more couples doing it? Going to the gym together, hiking, jogging, winter and summer sports, the list of activities can go on forever to suit each palate and level of ease or ruggedness. Whether you're an adventurer or a homebody, there are choices to fit you.

Engaging in physical activities together can release stress and strengthen the bond between you. And you can design how, any way that you like; but decide together.

Growing Together Mentally and Emotionally:

Let your partner in on your dreams and interests and be sensitive to hers as well. Your partner can be your cheerleader and give you the anchor that you may need to move forward.

Appreciation and validation of each other is empowering. Both of you reap the benefits. You feel closer and good about each other and about you. He also feels the same. With love and your partner as cheerleader in your corner, you have the belief and confidence to take risks and to follow your heart.
Lasting relationships boost each partner's morale when each person feels valued and dreams flourish.

Share the experiences and growth along the way. Yes, even if it's growing pains. They don't have to weaken what you already have together. Your relationship can be resilient even in the faces of adversity.

Growing Together Spiritually:

Spiritual growth has many meanings some of which include prayer, communion with God or a Higher Power, going to church, synagogue or meditation. Even planting and pruning your garden can take on a spiritual richness. Walking in nature and finding ways to get in touch with natural beauty can increase uplifting feelings for both of you. You are lifted out of yourself and into something profound.

When you do this together, whatever form you decide upon, something wonderful happens. As a result, your relationship deepens because you have opened soul to soul. You are in soulful communion with each other and with something beyond the two of you, something much more.

How To Love   Jo Anne White

Growing Together

→ Talk over ways that the two of you can grow together.

→ Maybe it's taking sailing or scuba diving lessons together.

→ Learn to cook gourmet meals, rehab a house or golf.

→ Sign up for the gym as a couple or schedule tango lessons. You decide.

→ Cultivate activities that you can share and that add to your mutual growth.

→ Find spiritual experiences like walking in nature, prayer, meditation and soulful music to bring you spiritually closer.

→ Take a course together or plan an adventurous trip.

→ Fix up a garden, a room, a house together with planning and collaboration.

97

Exercise 6:
How You Will Grow Together:

Discuss with your partner what you'll do to grow together.

Write it down.

_____

- _____
- _____
- _____
- _____
- _____
- _____
- _____

Chapter Seven:
Attracting Lasting Love

"Love is a choice you make from moment to moment."

Barbara De Angelis

Law of Attraction:

More and more people are catching on to the power of this universal principle that works whether or not you understand it. So why not let it work for you.

The Law of Attraction can work to change your circumstances whatever they are and can keep you on track with creating and maintaining a loving, healthy and supportive relationship.

Your thoughts are energy and are like magnets. They attract whatever you focus on whether it feels good to you or not. You'll get more of the same stuff in your life depending upon what you think about and how you feel.

Yes, your feelings are also powerful to bring to you whatever you want. Your thoughts and feelings work together to bring what you choose; that is if you're creating it. And unfortunately, they'll bring about what it is you don't want to attract just because you spend so much thinking time and feeling time on it.

You can change this at any time in your life and in your relationship. You can consciously decide what to attract and take steps to actively bring it in. You can program what you'd like to receive. Plan proactively to keep your relationship loving and close.

Relationship Visualization:

You know what feels good and you know how you want to be treated. You already feel good in this relationship and want those feelings to continue and be long-lasting. They can. I'll never suggest doing away with working cooperatively and consciously as a couple to keep the relationship strong.

Here's another method that can have profound and sometimes magical results and can bring about your future together.

Visualize it!

Yes that's right, with as much detail as you can muster, see in your mind's eye, the relationship thriving and strengthening. What does that look like to you? Create the pictures, the images of a loving relationship: happy faces, touching, laughing together, talking, sharing something special.

See all the elements in your mind, with your eyes open or closed. Practice this often and enjoy the experience. What can be even more special is to envision together, creating pictures aloud in your minds and discussing them.

Feel the Relationship Harmony:

Think healthy, happy, harmonious relationship thoughts and visualize them also, but that's not enough. You have to create feelings and emotions that feel like a loving happy relationship. You know how you feel when you feel loved and appreciated and when you feel the same way for your partner.

Conjure up those feelings of relationship success often. Attach them to the corresponding pictures and thoughts.
Do this over and over in your mind and in your feelings. Imagine all of the loving taking place right now in the present and continuing into the future. Feel what those feelings are like inside you, in your body and mind and see yourself with those feelings.

Belief:

Believe that it will happen and trust that it will happen without worrying. Don't question or concern yourself with how you're going to keep the relationship thriving. Just know that you are and you will.

The energy of thought, especially loving, upbeat thought is very powerful. So instead of dwelling on what you are momentarily dissatisfied about in the relationship or in your partner, change your thinking.

Change your feeling and change your pictures. Change them to how you'd like him to behave toward you or how you'd like the relationship to progress and they will.

Although your relationship is loving and upbeat, now, still use the Law of Attraction and the necessary steps to keep it the way you want it for now and into the future.

With the Law of Attraction on your side, you both are unstoppable. You'll attract more loving opportunities and experiences together and for each other. What's more, you'll feel good while you're doing it and feel even better as they happen.

Exercise 7: Love Attraction

1. Remind yourself of what you enjoy in your partner, your relationship and you, and how you feel in partnership.

2. Focus on loving thoughts and specific images or pictures.

   For example, see the two of you buying a house together or laughing together or holding hands or whatever you like.

3. You choose the images and the thoughts that suit you best and that signify relationship bliss for you.

4. Do this often. You can repeat the same images or create new ones. Keep the focus on the feelings and pictures that signal to your mind what you want.

5. Trust that it will come about.

6. Do this relationship envisioning activity together. Create the images and feelings with your partner at the same time.

   Share aloud what you are each creating for you both. Share the enthusiasm, joy and excitement together too.

Nurture you and your partner in the relationship and ask for what you need. Nurture the relationship by paying attention to the good qualities of the relationship and thinking about it and about the two of you together with enthusiasm and expectancy.

With open dialogue, sharing and your commitment, your relationship will be enriched by the new experiences as well as the challenges. Think of them as opportunities to strengthen your love. And they will!

Together in Growth:

Laugh Together

Share Together

Play Together

Plan Together

Explore Together

Solve Together

Visualize Together

Imagine Together

Be in Silence Together

Be Soulful Together

About The Author:

Relationship expert, Dr. Jo Anne White is an author, international speaker, life coach and therapist.

Her relationship advice had been sought after by live radio and television audiences such as CN8 and NBC.

For over twenty years, Dr. White has helped thousands of men and women overcome personal and professional challenges and find direction and success in their lives. She has helped couples find more relationship satisfaction.

Dr. White is a professional motivational and keynote speaker. She has been featured in magazines and newspapers throughout the United States and Canada some of which include Match.com, House and Garden, Woman's World and WebMD.

You are invited to check out more relationship e-books, as well as other products and seminars developed by Dr. White.

Visit: **http://www.drjoannewhite.com** for more life affirming products and information.

Visit: **www.docwhite.org**. to read more inspirational articles and news.

Call **1-877-Doc White** for more information.

To Contact Dr. Jo Anne White directly:

Call: 1-877-Doc White or Write:

PO Box 176
Haddonfield, NJ
08033

Remember that Dr. White is available for private and confidential consultations about you and your relationship.

She has helped many couples get their relationships back on track and has helped thousands of men and women realize their potential, reach their dreams and live with more life balance and satisfaction.

Please check out Dr. White's other books, CD's and products designed with you in mind.

www.docwhite.org

Also by Dr. Jo Anne White

Sense Your Way to Life Satisfaction

Surviving a Breakup: Your Guide to Recovery

Breaking Up: Letting Go with Grace

CD's & Programs

Focus on Success

Journey into Relaxation

Total Sense®: Life Success Programs, CD's, & Seminars

www.ingramcontent.com/pod-product-compliance
Lightning Source LLC
LaVergne TN
LVHW011405080426
835511LV00005B/415